IMPOSSIBLE FLYING

ALSO BY KWAME DAWES

POETRY

Resisting the Anomie
Progeny of Air
Prophets
Jacko Jacobus
Requiem
Shook Foil
Mapmaker
Midland
New and Selected Poems
Bruised Totems
Wisteria Twilight Songs from the Swamp Country
I Saw Your Face

ANTHOLOGIES

Wheel and Come Again: An Anthology of Reggae Poetry

FICTION

A Place to Hide
Bivouac (forthcoming)

NONFICTION

Natural Mysticism: Towards a New Reggae Aesthetic
Talk Yuh Talk: Interviews with Anglophone Caribbean Poets
Bob Marley: Lyrical Genius
Twenty: South Carolina Poetry Fellows
A Far Cry from Plymouth Rock: A Personal Narrative

IMPOSSIBLE FLYING
Poems

KWAME DAWES

PEEPAL TREE

First published in Great Britain in 2007, reprinted 2010
Peepal Tree Press Ltd
17 King's Avenue
Leeds LS6 1QS
UK

ISBN: 9 781 84523 039 5

Supported by
ARTS COUNCIL
ENGLAND

CONTENTS

Four: Switch

Five: Mistake

for
Kojo, Aba, Adjoa, Gwyneth, Kojovi
for
Mama the Great
for
Sena, Kekeli and Akua
and for
Lorna for being there always
Remembering
Neville

ONE

LEGEND

LEGEND

For Kojovi

A deep pink face webbed in canary-yellow netting,
swaddled in infant finery — flesh soft to the eye.
This is how we first met; you, unblinking,

a week old, and the order of my life shifted.
I was four and you seemed outside of me,
outside of meaning. The nine months before

were blank, no recollection of waiting
for what must have been our mother's
marvellously round body. For it to turn

to this. At four, I stared at the full-length
mirror, then sprinted to the back of it
to find my revenant. My first inexplicable

equation: the hide-and-seek of my image.
How easily it slipped away. At four,
all was accommodation of mysteries, a new baby

the advent of snails after rain, the wide
valley of guinea-pig grass — a green, fluent sea
on which our cement and glass house sailed;

the magic appearance and disappearance
of this man, Neville, our father who grinned
while bearing you like he did gifts

from exotic ports; smiling proudly
with that familiar gap-tooth and mischievous
eyes gray as a blind man's marble eye;

bearing you, his lump of pink flesh,
eyes tightly shut, fingers curled.
Now the world had changed as worlds must.

THE USURPER ARRIVES

Beyond the house afloat on the undulation of bush,
(the green is dense tall grasses of savannah land – the earth

metallic orange) the hill's face rises like a gentle wave
of unseen brush and bramble interrupted

by miniature bungalows, their roofs dark tiled
as natural as the bark of trees, the tough husk

of giant shac-shac pods. Then, more tangled vegetation;
the sharp grey-white of tawny branches

with vicious needles, the final passage before the even hedges
of Mensah Saba Hall, the clock, the pinkish brown walls,

the ivory face, the peak, jutting into the unflinching
blue sky. We lived in a world of gigantic anthills,

a world of tough soil, open fields, derelict cars,
and a landscape so brittle, a mere toying with flame

could set the place ablaze. To this first home
you came, usurper of all I surveyed.

TYPE

All is glitter and clean, white cement spotted by buffed
pebbles; metal, glass, porcelain — the tiles, this sixties modernity —
the louvres of green glass causing the unwavering blue light
to pattern the floor with a cool underwater mosaic.
The yolky dying of everything; the trees, the marl
driveway, the rough cement walls, dusting them with a plague
of gold, like pollen or something less wholesome — insecticide.

Somewhere in this light, the hall empties, the guests
have departed, some lingering in the driveway,
laughing, warm with spirits. You came down to mimic
the gestures of adults; moving from table
to table, from coaster to coaster, sipping the icy dregs left
for the gods — the good whiskey, gin, cognac, *akpeteshi*;
the metallic edge of such sweet aromas. You drank
until you collapsed where we found you, in the middle
of tables and chairs, drunk as a lord, so vocally drunk,
you spoke like an Ashanti chief, as though somewhere
you had met one, poured libation with one, chewed
kola nut with one — laughing, slapping your thighs:
Bring me my chokota! How bolstered you were by the liquor;
how bewildered we were staring at your man's way.
We wanted to serve.

The panic, the sudden fear of not knowing you,
the tightening of my stomach, Mama's guilt-ridden
energy, our father's bemused uncertainty,
his arms dangling, seem too familiar now;
the first rituals, really, of our later catastrophes.

MASTER MIND

We invested the power of invention – creation, even –
in you. Watching you take shape, we imagined how
we could make you better than we were – so pure,
so much a seed or (a better metaphor) raw clay;

each utterance, each leap, each engagement with the world,
our discovery of perfection. We saw you as malleable
(see how well the metaphor works?) the one who would
become an athlete, strong, trained, made into a tool

of mastery and we would shape you. When you found
language, it was so miraculous the way words spun around
in your head – four jabbering siblings all trying
to feed you with songs, with Mark Antony's speech

fed by us uncomprehending mimics, riding the iambics
like babblers looking for the anchor of meter,
and when you returned them, with such comprehension
in your eyes; when you drew figures that looked

like forms we could recognize (and how we read
the entrails of your scribbles, discovering portents
of greatness in the tiniest markings) we were convinced
of your genius. We crowned you precocious carrier

of all our myths: Our *Master Mind*, here at last!
And you wore it with the ease of a second name.
Such lofty expectations – the stuff of memoirs
had we been better tutors, less self-indulgent,

more studied, persistent. Our demands
were impossible; and eventually you too dreamed
of genius like a birthright, an uneasy band
tightening around your expanding forehead.

WHISPERERS

In Hounslow for a brief spell, we squatted
in the basement of a Barbadian who may have owed
my father some favour. His settling of debts,
(something perhaps like an Oxford obligation)
was a basement of three dank rooms, a toilet,
and a tyrannical landlord's rules. We whispered,
always whispered tensely in the basement, afraid
to embarrass the old man.

We whispered about being superheroes and flying.
We drafted in detailed colour our supermobile;
each part scavenged from everyday things –
even the mechanics were pragmatic physics, not
fantasy, but something we thought we could make,
a tank able to traverse wide open fields.
We hoarded garbage bags, secreting them under
our beds, these to be made into tightfitting
supercostumes. It was all devised in white silence.

Upstairs, the man's sons played with matchbox cars.
Downstairs we played with matchboxes, matches,
each burnt-up tip a man's head.

Twice weekly, at twilight, on family walks
we followed the undulation of these gentle valleys,
our calm, tree-full accommodations, where the pavements,
stained with dogshit and rusty leaves, marked order
and the civility of country living.
Perhaps we were meant to cut loose, run,
screaming our liberation to the open air
after being penned in decorous silence so long;
but we bowed heads and whispered, conspiring.

TWO

IMPOSSIBLE FLYING

ESTIMATED PROPHET
...preacher preaching on the burning shore
(Grateful Dead via Burning Spear)

I am no apostle to this city – but I carry
a gospel in my head. I wear righteousness
like sin forgiven, and on evenings red
and steamy like this, the city a crowding
of sweaty bodies, I cradle prophecies, heavy
truths of God's schemes in my head. On the bus
from Half-Way-Tree, this healing flame
tingles the tips of my fingers. This old
earth, this old city, this road of sticky
asphalt, this coffin of black people:
O Kingston – no sunlight, no beach music,
just the daily routine of folks hustling a living.

I sit in the heat like a prophet should,
carrying the earth in my brain – the bus
shuddering its way through the dust and exhaust
on Hope Road with the mountains looming
and the road cutting through the plain,
then rising up towards the cool hills.
Tonight, I meet the fear that will haunt me
with faith and the terror of a family
rupturing. In my mind it is a normal day,
and I long to say hello to you, my shadow,
the boy with laughter in each word,
the boy whose eyes are mine. I long
to knuckle your knuckles, laugh at your stories
and walk away with love. But today,
I meet you crumbled against the rusting bell.
You have no name, no language,
just the dull eyes of a stranger.

RESURRECTION

After the year of cataclysm, the walls of this city
are scarred with green and red hieroglyphs of hate,
the tragic lies of false prophets; the rubble,
the stones, the air still thick with last breaths –
800 blasted lives – and palms and bells, rods
and anthems strewn around, the detritus
of a celebration we won't ever understand.
We have bled out our peace. Those nights
we trembled, remember? The righteous
and the fallen have fled. The city
is dusty and broken after years of neglect.
How we suffered for a dream, recycled
our glad rags for the simpler things –
such sacrifices we made in that valiant,
austere decade. The season of cataclysm
still haunts our city, and we dance
our spastic Restoration, a world of vain
hope: the coke, the untrammelled
sex, and into this world shadows
steal across our secret pleasures.
So little to love. I travel
this city with a stone for a tongue,
watching the light of a new moon.
I travel this road, with the limp of a survivor;
sometimes the backfire of a car leaves me
washed with fear, my heart and head pulsing.
I walk into the gate of my *alma mater* –
once my sanctuary from the city – now alien;
it has been a year and everything seems
so trite, so malformed and rough hewn.
I pass through the rusting gates
framed by the languorous ficus berry trees;

the sound of an old doomsday hymn,
the schoolboy contraltos lamenting in my head.
Dear Jesus, this place smells
of revival and death. I come through the gate
with faith – tomorrow it shall be tested.
Holy Spirit, breathe on me, breathe on me!
It is six and dusk; Simms Building is alabaster
in the gloom – this golden deadness
is the sepulchre of the unrisen dead. I find you,
Master Mind, leaning against the tongueless bell.

IMPOSSIBLE FLYING

"Palms of Victory/ Deliverance is here!"
1980 Jamaica Labour Party campaign song

1

On Kingston's flat worn earth,
everything is hard as glass.
The sun smashes into the city – no breath,
no wind, just the engulfing, asthmatic noonday.

We move with the slow preservation
of people saving their strength
for a harsher time. 1980:
this land has bled – so many betrayals –
and the indiscriminate blooding of hope
has left us quivering, pale,
void, the collapsed possibilities
causing us to limp. We are a country
on the edge of the manic euphoria
of a new decade: Reagan's nodding
grin ripples across the basin's
surface. We dare to dream
that in the spin and tongues of Kapo
perhaps we too will fly this time,
will lift ourselves from the slough
of that dream-maker's decade –
the '70s when we learned things only
before suspected: our capacity for blood,
our ability to walk through a shattered
city, picking our routine way to work
each morning. We are so used now to the ruins,

perhaps more than that, perhaps to wearing
our sackcloth and ash as signs of our
hope, the vanity of survival.

In that decade when a locksman
could prance the streets with a silver
magic trail in his wake, how we fought
to be poor, to be sufferers, to say
Looking at you the better one; how
we cultivated our burden-bearing,
white-squall, hungry belly,
burlap-wearing, Cariba-suited
socialist dream; how reggae
with its staple of faith, fame
and fortune spoke its revelation
from the speakers of souped-up
BMWs. Gone now, all gone.

We have thrown off that dead skin now;
and the fleets of squat Ladas
are rusting, O Havana.
We've grown too cynical for such austerity
or perhaps we did not suffer enough.
So on such blank and startled days, we dream
of flight. How we hope: *Dance!*
Dance, damn it! Dance, damn it! Be happy!
Our apocalypse echoes on the sound system
and we dance. These laws, these new laws,
these palm leaves, these clamouring bells,
so desperate for deliverance,
this insipid green in the future, and we all
stare at the unflinching sky
and will our hearts to fly.

And how you ran, sprinting
down Carlisle Avenue,
your face set against the bare wind;

you were spreading your arms
undulating in complete faith
in the wind's lift,

the physics of the updraft;
past the low fences,
the skittish yelping dogs,

the streaks of telephone wires,
the hibiscus hedges
a blur of green and pink

and smudged off-white;
and me calling you,
trying hard to bring you back;

me catching up,
behind you now, our heat,
our panting, the slap of bare feet

on the soft asphalt;
and I reached for you,
held you by the waist,

drawing you down;
and it felt in that instant
not like a shattering of faith

but a struggle to keep
you home, for each tendon
of your body throbbed

with the lightness of a body
prepared for flight.
And my betrayal was to become

the burden,
the anchor you had
for years longed to shake off.

Stillness, the gaping crowd
staring at this sudden accident:
two men in a heap

of twisted limbs
on the road;
you saying, *This time, this time,*

this time if you had let me,
it would have happened.
I too felt the vanity

of our beaching.
The bells shimmered;
the dispatches were in:

No one
was flying
no more.

BIRTHRIGHT

1

The narrative is a myth, not history, not in the blood:
the cricket, the books, the poems, the stories,
the lovers (such unfaithfulness), the instinctive
charm, long letters, the tongue of seduction:
all of these as if the blood carries sin
from generation to generation. But it is all myth,
an inheritance stolen on some careless night
in Mandeville. A man dying. A son caught mourning
in the slow-moving air. A wife hymning
this death watch. It is as if something
is being passed on. The thing is, I was there,
and no one else made it, and I took what I could
in that hour of lamentation. There in that night,
the green city so dark it turned everything
into a deep unmoving space, I looked again
at that photo and accepted the imputed glory.

Now, twenty years later, I return to that sepia photo
of two men walking along the Thames,
somewhere near a chapel, the BBC behind them,
with its dark cold studios where in that hour
at the microphone, they smelt the humid
saltiness of their island. For that quiet hour
they deposited love in the cadence of their island
talk. Then it turned into painful nostalgia
and longing in the sudden blast of the air off the river,
the stench of history and dog shit on the long street
beside the ornate chapel (grey, stolid against a pewter
sky); beside the statue of horses with straining muscles
and grimaces; beside the square spared by the Luftwaffe;

the geriatric empire whose doddering they called
a well-preserved swagger (they were still believers).

The two men are walking towards the camera
with the wind flapping their baggy trousers
around their thin legs. On the left is our father —
so odd that he is younger than I am now,
and I want to mistake him for me.
But at his age, sandals, worn corduroys were my uniform,
and the dust and bush of UWI, my haunts.
Besides, he is thin (*these minor famines*,
says Swanzy, the BBC chap), which makes him
fit-looking. Hunger is a constant condition,
the uniform of the desperate artist like the narrow tie,
billowing slacks, the tweed, tailored jacket
with leather elbow-patches, the empty pipe.
His eyes, his scraggly beard, his bright gaze
are thirsty for a pint and carefree laughter.
Let's say it as simply as we must — I see you.

2

This is *your* inheritance. I have stolen
much, first the photo, and then the idea
of the photo, as if that was me by the Thames.
But *what is fe yuh cyaan un-fe-yuh.*

I am the counterfeit inheritor, fortunate
to have been at the right place when these things
were given out. Ask Jacob. It was never
diabolic and he, like me, had God or chance to blame.

But I am the wrong corpus for the melancholic
blue notes of a heart so broken, so hidden –
the language you understand so well.

And this was his vernacular, the complex
in those eyes bulbous and bright against the grey
of London. Me, I am the caretaker, the keeper
of secrets, the one who borrowed his wisdom
and art and wore it well. These things I have taken
as if they were mine. I can't be blamed.
Even *he* thought me the heir; even *he* longed
to make me the sequel. It was arranged,
the cricket, the school, the English literature,
the big talk of Oxford, because we all believed.

But you, tipsy with your insanities, you have known
it all along, though for years stayed silent
until that dark shed with the lizards
and the haunting broke something in you.
It is the way of narratives of blood,
that are untidily ribboned in old myths.
It is the way of stolen birthrights, the messy
contracts we make with blood legacies.

VERNACULAR

On a sunset beach at summer's end, a man
balances the judgment of the world on the tips
of his outstretched hands: a flirtation
with the language of damnation and salvation.
A lover enacts a myth — an old narrative that love,
too, in the face of gaunt death, is possible —
how trite, how Paul McCartney, all that fluff.
TV tragedy is reliable for its arcs, its tears,
its climaxes at quarter to, its tidy denouements.
So I make stanzas of a man dying of AIDS,
his lover buoyant, the golden hour at hand,
and I write of you, of brothers who love.

Two brothers wrestle like lovers.
They are in their parents' marriage bed
where all mystery was discarded so long
ago and what is left is the security
of entwined smells, the smells of love —
a woman's intimate muskiness and flowers,
a man's old sweat and clean gin cool.
They are too young to know the taboo, too caught up
in the riot of their blood to translate the idioms
of eroticism. What is left is the memory
of bonds, like the secret of how we grew
to rely on the smell of sweat in our clothes.
I can tell he is my brother by his smell.

This is the tale of our redemption.
We are grown men, now. Fathers,
we have planted our seed, written poems,
made love, held the body of an aging parent,
whispered secrets, tumbled back

into a scattering of tongues, dry leaves stirring.
The memory is as fine as the day
it happened in the green filtered light
of Neville and Mama's room; the coolest
room with windows crowded by crotons
and hibiscuses garlanded by giddy
hummingbirds. That room of cool comforts:
Old Spice, make-up talc, and Noxema.
Neville is dead now, and I don't shave
so I have no use for the off-white flasks
of Old Spice. We do die. It is the way
of the world, it is how myths are made.

A man on TV turns in the sand – a gay white man
I would never know or like – but his poem
carries to me quietly, a universe in words,
a vernacular I understand as mine, the dialect
of two men loving, not lovers, but brothers,
crossing time with memory and haunting.

PRE-MORTEM
For Neville

1

I have tried to recall this as one would seasons,
but the island is a monotone of sun and occasional
rain, rapid and consuming — everything softening
before the hard light of an eleven o'clock sun.
It may have been April — for the poetry of it, I pluck
it, dangle it, adorn it with the Easter sermons
of spilt blood seeping from the A.M. radio.
In Kingston, after the clutter of traffic dies
down, after I turn into the tree-thick Avenue
off Barbican Road, late at night, the street
a black disquiet stretching into the hills,
the sound of an old transistor carries like sound
under water. The sharp orange spot
of light moves in slow arches. A ritual
as comforting as meditation is being enacted.
The scent of Rothmans meets me — it is as if
I am in another place, high in the St. Ann Hills,
Sturge Town, your town where you tasted
first fruit, where the voices of old once-
slaves moved through the black nights
repeating the secrets of duppies, long-tongued,
sweet-toothed phantoms that sipped the drip
of molasses easing its smooth way through
the cured wooden barrels knocking against
the soggy deck of the rocking cart: Hear 'im:
If de molasses so sweet, how tas'e de sugar?
I find you on the verandah, B.T. Williams
grinding out his sermons, and my brother,
your son, sits beside you. Together,

you listen to these sermons as if you have come
to church to find in this forgiving darkness
grace, salvation, peace and forgiveness
for those years of faithlessness — the pragmatic
suspension of belief in the Marxist dream.

2

The power has been down for hours, the candles
have melted and cooled to hard puddles
in the Milo tin covers, and I sense that you two —
old man and boy, once strangers and now
friends, equals, co-conspirators in the dark —
are negotiating how to share the acts of care Mama
offers. She is mothering both of you now.
The chemicals have slowed the younger,
and despair in this new season
of unemployment, dreams souring
and the absence of poems, letters, novels
have halted the elder. I imagine now, jealously,
what secrets you are sharing, what stories,
what lies, what silences, what tears.
I do not stay with you. I cannot.
Instead, I walk into the pause, then,
stumbling into the humid house,
I hear the rush of whispers and chuckles
fill the vacuum of my wake. I know
that in this I have found the mystery of his calm
acceptance when you died those months
later, in another season, on another familiar night.

ODE TO THE AMERICAN DREAM

On this island, where the dream of incredible
heroics from the squalor of a mundane life
is not a part of our dialect, our geniuses
walk ordinary paths through a people
that does not cheer, hoot, adore. The fall
is unremarkable here, while in that other country,
where the dream is a tenet of faith,
your devotion to making songs
would have been the natural discourse.
On the island you imagined
yourself juke-jointing in Memphis,
twisting your body around a microphone,
a swell of bodies reaching for you.
You filled page after page with the simple
hooks of pop songs – tunes we had no language
to describe or embrace. We had no language,
no head to see in you something that could leap
from the ordinary into the remarkable.
We were hardly the dreamers, mavericks,
quixotic clowns reminding a nation that magic happens
even here in these monotonous tropics.
Our sin was not mere benign indifference,
it was worse, it was unbelief, the tragic
foolishness of doubt, and we tried to show
you reality, to say that none of us,
ordinary, reasonable people, so grounded
in irony and an acute affliction of truth,
could be superstars. Our labours
to make our convictions truth in you
must have been enough to shatter
your mind and worse, your heart.

WARD

The dirt track turns to marl in the wind tunnel
between Maternity – the pale yellow gowns of swollen
women, a constant slash of light through the gray
louvres – and the whitewashed ward where you are.
My heart grows as I walk by casually,
trying to pretend I have forgotten your eyes pleading
with me in the brightly lit greeting room,
pointing to the stumble and glossolalia
of the pretty girl who does not care that her breasts
are poking out of the too small hospital issue
green tunic. Around us the sterile slow pace
of medicated bodies. Like her, I imagine
that you don't belong; I imagine you are too
astute, too collected for this; your pathologies
are civil things. And yet I see the scars
on your knuckles, and you drool, how you drool,
your tongue, not yours, just a clumsy lump
of meat in your mouth. You are telling me you need
to go, lucid as anyone I know, until you laugh,
reminding me of the morning I held you down,
tied your wings, did not have the faith;
and in that same clean logic, your eyes
stared steadily at me as you spoke in soft
conspiracy, *I woulda be flying now,*
you know that? I woulda be flying if you never
hold me down… It has been a week
since I stopped. That last time the orderlies
told me of the straps you strained against,
the electricity, the padded walls, the shit
in your pants, the tears, as if you were
someone else, as if they needed me
to understand the lunatic's dialect, as if

they saw in me the hubris of class, or the hope
of sanity; as if I did not understand
the commonness of tragedy. That day I did not stop.
I simply bowed my head and walked away
weeping, angry at my tears, at the noble sorrow –
as if it was me caught in this wrestle
with the chemistry of the head – the demon tyranny.
I wept (a good verb) like an actor, testing each mood,
swept, yes, by the passion of the narrative,
but consumed by the tragic consequence
of fear. I wept as I walked the stony path
to Papine, helpless like that. Tonight
is the seventh night I have walked past.
It becomes easier, now. I fear only
that you will see me going by, not stopping.
Maybe you will see my lips moving, praying
for the miracle promised – another vanity –
the scripted prophecy of my peace.

CASTING OUT DEMONS

From the cave, a laugh gurgles, surfaces.
You have learned the dialect of my prayers,
a lingo of rules. You laugh, I cast it out;
they are legion; they keep returning.
I came to see you in the daytime, for despite
my faith I fear the terror of night, the way
sudden light plays on my nerves. I imagine your
valley: the gloom, you wondering about
tomorrow: impossible equations. A week
ago, I dragged you from the toilet. I thought
I would find you bleeding. You were only
crying. I reached. You held me, crushing me.

We trained you well. A ball smashed
over the fence and you always were our
emissary, the one to plead. You always were
the tester of waters, the one to ask the old man
for the hard things, to face wrath, to face the gloom
we feared and the blow of denial
with the genius art of tears and the open-
faced plea of the perpetual infant.
He never said no. You think it nothing
now to sail through this, as if
in no time you will come back grinning,
rewarded with the ball in hand.

I pray over your shining forehead.
Your arms are sinew lined; you are
a thinner version of me and not strange enough
for the necessary detachment of strangers.
It is easier to cast out demons
from strangers because I am unfamiliar

with the line separating personalities,
who is to know the demon from the host,
or the evidence of true healing –
a righted mind – in a stranger?
My faith is not tested by the logic
of psychology. It is all spirit and fire.

I mutter my tongues sluggish like the thick
stale air in the room. I am waiting for them
to catch aflame, grow wings, to make
your head light, clean, to return you to the boy
who used to laugh with me for hours
over a single image of Roman foot soldiers,
swatted by Asterix and Obelix, their sandals
suspended like an empty coil of leather –
the look of comic violence – how we laughed.
The boy is gone. I want to find him,
but you are growing too quickly for him.
To return would be to retard all love – the beard,
the voice, the dropping of fat, the age
in your eyes. Sometimes I see the fear,
as if so far in the recess of your cave,
you are trying to say something,
trying to grant me the faith to believe.

1980

The days are shadows. The old man in worn shorts
with ashen knees limps into the gloom; his body
is shrinking – how quickly age comes on us, comes

on the heart broken by loss of all good things. The year
of cataclysm – a nation changes direction and labels
its new monsters. In months, his blood thickens,

turns sluggish – a tiny series of explosions burst in his brain.
He is sharp as always, but words come in slurs
and time is best spent as an invalid incapable of peace.

A man loses his job in this country at this edge
of history when the world is cut through by
competing loyalties (*If they are not with us, they are*

against us, says the Patriarch with a movie star's
cultivated gravitas) and his friends forsake him
like rats slouching from a listing barge.

He looks to the sunlight letting its rays shine
hard into his eyes, as if to defy the splendour of fate.
You broke in that year – broke into a foundering

incoherence and his body could not find the language
for peace or comfort. When a father has no answers,
something dies in him. Now a brooding silence
shadows the man in this dull dawn of his fading.

SECRETS

So young you learned the entrapment of secrets.
Your history is scattered across the city;
even strangers have seen you stumble, your heartbeat
echoing in your head. They have shown pity
and collected your story; given you food
like alms for the poor. You dignify their pity.
On better days you walk the roads naked;
everyone knows you, knows of you. How easily
you laugh, not stalked by the fear of being revealed.
Who can hold threats over you? *Splashing good!*
you say, laughing, *Splashing good!* You let
it all hang out there. No mystery of your blood
is buried, no sin, no failing, no cheating,
no indiscretion, no embarrassment. It is all
out there, the life without secrets, a superstar's
life. So young, you have learned the tyranny
of discretion, learned to shun it — a simple lesson
I have learned only too late and with pain.
I have lived all turned in on myself, like a poem
trying to see the grace of a mountain's face,
but only caught up in the twisted entanglement
of roots imprisoned in the clay of myth:
my decency, my sanity, the lie of my life.
I am wracked now with the purest envy
for you whose liberty flits windily about you.

WHEN MARXISTS PRAY

1

We gather to pray, passing invocations
around the cramped room, voice after voice
asking for mercy. Today, though, the ritual

atheist silence after the sixth
is broken by his voice,
baritone and tattered

at the edges. He prays
and grows small enough
to believe that a prayer

will turn things around;
small enough, to return, prodigal,
to the quiet chapel on the hill

above his home in Sturge Town,
where sturdier faith thrived
in his proud ancestry.

2

He prays and the ordinary dwarfs him.
This man shrinks, losing the quixotic
aura of dreams: *A cottage, a lovely cottage*
in Oxford, my children around me, my poems,
my son healed, cricket every Sunday on the green.
And help us to be a family, help us…
In my weakness, in my splendid weakness.

3

We say *Amen*, collect our plates and eat.

Everything tastes like dust.

THREE

ANATOMY OF ANGER

There is a moment
A tip in time
When leaving home
is the lesser crime...

Paul Simon

BRIGHT EYES

1

The woman is a poet.
Her hair is a medusa head
of greying tendrils.

Her body caves in on itself
at each hacking cough,
each phlegm-clogged wracking.

She strains to take air
into lungs that have lost their use.
Her mouth hangs open to pant.

The cigarette smoke leaves a perfume
of decay on her skin.
The woman is a metaphor.

Her body is collapsing, her mind
is broken. I am holding her,
while she shakes.

Maybe it is just
this bleak Bristol air,
or the recurring prophecies

of March — a ritual
she anticipates and is seduced by.
So I hold her, thinking of you.

It has been a decade
since you took those pills
she will not take.

I am ashamed
of how easily I unfold from her
and scuttle off for help.

3

A poet died alone
in her London bedsit.
It was winter. For five weeks

she sat in her living room,
the music on the CD turning
and turning. A famous poet.

Dead five weeks
before they found her.
These deafening metaphors

are not about poetry –
hardly the point – they are
reminders of what love is.

No more poems.
They always find a way.
They outlast everything,
cynical to the last foot.

WASPS
Road Town, Tortolla

1

A tribe of golden wasps has occupied the brightly lit
room with its grand windows looking out into the tiny
fenced-off botanical garden where teenagers grope

at night, school uniforms lifted, crumpled, their hearts
racing at these clandestine acts. This is my mother's
room and we have come to this island, a year after

the quiet ceremony and the sweet assurances
of first marriage, to find something of a cliché
of beach and sun. Fredericton is still frozen

in late April. I have not seen you in years.
You are gaunt, your body taut with casual labour.
So far, you have survived those menial duties.

The voice of Neville, his cultured authority
(a peculiar inheritance), boomed abuse at the white
bastards you had to serve in this tourist nest.

Now you guard a factory with a billy-club,
and pragmatic fear (*I tell them take what
they want and I run if needs be. I just make*

alarm — not no superhero. Dem days done.)
You are getting better. Heroics were a symptom,
a kind of euphoric lack of judgment — impossible

strength. Flying in, before seeing you, I worried:
the gap, the ocean, the time, my betrayals,
as if I had planted another wall between us.

These things loom over our meeting,
but we embrace, laughing, almost in tears,
two big men, no more little brother, big brother.

2

Perhaps we can breathe now, I think.
At night, the wasps descend, get tangled
in sheets, and I am stung, sharp and lasting.

We abandon the room for the moonlight
and sweaty air of the verandah — the sound
of the ocean thumping, the occasional light

squall spitting welcome cool drops — the heat,
the frogs, the crickets, the furtive whisper
of lovers in the public garden below.

We make love in the sticky heat, quietly, my arrival
a weight, like all my pleasures when I think of you
sleeping through dreams, my laughter

slipping into tears. I hold her, try to assure
myself that I deserve this, this love, this joy,
while the sting of these wasps pulses in my neck.

YOUR HANDS
for Mama

A mother cradles her child even when the head
grows too cumbersome for embrace – and you,

who remain constant through these years,
it is hard to make poems for you since I come

always as a heavy head longing to be soothed.
It is mother love, I have learned: the tenderness

of your sculptor's palms greasy with Vicks
on my skin; the gentle intrusion of your fingers

searching my bowels for maddening worms;
the quick brush of your massage slick with pink

lotion, softening the itchy cracked sores of the pox;
the calming voice, never panicked even when

I walked in at two in the morning, my body
splotched with welts the size of an open palm

from eating ten too many crab cakes (*If it has
not killed you yet, it won't – go to sleep*).

Still, after years, after imagining that I have
deserved your grace for my 'good son' ways,

it is clear to me now that you always knew me
for the fragile child I was, the careful manager

of my pathologies, the marathon masturbation
binges, the secreted clandestine letters to lovers,

52

the fear of the dark, the terror of failure;
and yet you have loved, and what you have

loved has never changed: my infant, my heart,
my navel string, the umbilicus that ties me

to you, to home, to Ghana, to the instant
when the impossible pain of childbirth

propelled me out; and then those five seasons
when I was the washbelly, the last child,

the baby. This love was built on the sacramental
truth of those years. Your hands moulded

my flesh, understanding the pressure of skin
on skin. And it makes sense that you would

love him, the one who came after – love him
through everything, like you have loved me,

for that love, too, was shaped in the basic
fluid and pain of birthing. How you love

is myth as simple as rainfall and dew at dawn.
My arrogance is my millstone, and until

this stumbling into tears and the hunger
for forgiveness and love,

I had not grasped the memory of your clay-
covered hands, the familiar intimacy of your touch.

BROTHER LOVE

It is familiar soil: the constancy of the hills
there each morning; the rituals of burying the dead —
the sound of names not heard for years on the radio,
the constant tragedy of their sudden passing;
the smell of food — oily, coconut-sweet,
thick, wafting through the heat from the mango
tree-darkened cluster of wood houses;
prayers as revealing as gossip in the congregation
of boredom: we are doing it all together.
These things are lost in exile
and it *is* exile, this awayness, this freedom
where we are fluttering in the wind with no reliable
anchor.
           My brother, we are strangers sometimes,
growing in our own locked worlds.
Then in a Kingston sunset, you knock fists with me
and turn into the boyish grinner for an instant.
I rediscover your brilliant eyes and we laugh
at the familiar code of silence, knowing, knowing
not to question it, but to hold on to
our shared history, the comfort of laughter,
the security of a desperately tight embrace;
knowing that it is in these tiny instances that we find
we have grown together despite the miles and years.

SOUTHERN LENT
Columbia, South Carolina

I have been waiting for this season;
now it is here, dull as a Monday morning.
The heat came overnight, and now the leprosy
of Easter speckles the dogwoods.

Assembly Street is elegant as a Chinese garden.
Healing, true healing is as painful as our ailments;
the body is shocked by the change, our native cancer
scraped viciously from our clinging flesh.

These fleeting moments: something beautiful
in this cruel earth. There is dignity and grace
in this place, and this year I learned,
in the new season, the language of mercy,
grace and forgiveness.

Here, feet buried in the carpet of petals,
I feel the weight of my guilt, stare through the naked grey
limbs into a blue brilliant sky and I know
that despite the sadness, hope will grow
and this season will come again, surprising
as Monday, freshly dying, restoring
the tenderness of our lives.

Tomorrow, I leave for Kingston.
You will be there, and I will not share this poem
with you. It is all hackneyed truth for you who know
too well the dialect of suffering and grace.

ANATOMY OF ANGER

With strangers my right eye jumps. The temper
is a red ball deep in my stomach — not clenching
of fists, nothing but the sickening rush of blood,
the suggestion of tears and the staggering voice.
I discover the genius of my anger
when it is too late. The aftermath is deflation,
the helpless sorrow of a body not used to having
its own way. Anger is an alien mood; it visits
and stays restless under my skin, nothing fits —
that is, with strangers. But perhaps I have
rehearsed this anger for years, carried it as a weight,
a final act, after years of restraint and hope.
Now that it is here, here on this tiny island,
the sun big over the sea, the miniature roads
bare at five-fifteen, all traffic gone, the voices
carrying into this overheated room,
the sound of steel drums pinging,
rehearsing eight months before the bacchanal
season, in this serenity, my anger feels old.
I wear it easily, calmly, fist tight. I could hit
now, hit as if I have always wondered
whether it could be beaten out of you,
beaten, this blight, this cruel edge, this unreasonable
callousness. I am calm, yet I understand
the calm of blood acts. I dare you; you come
forward, you punch; my chest accepts
easily; no pain. I know I can take anything
from you, like the big brother baring his stomach,
saying, *Punch it, punch it hard, punch it*. Again,
you punch — a dull force. I am sitting suddenly
in the chair. There is a history here.
You have longed to do this very thing, to beat

it out of me – the calm, the arrogance, the success,
the goodness, the lie – and staring at your looming
fury, I accept the logic: *He must kill me.*
He must kill me so I can be free of my shadow,
so he can be lighter. And this logic drowns
my wife saying no, my mother saying no.
All I can hear are the shits, the fucks,
the bitches, the bloodclaats, the spittle raining
on me, and I say, *Kill me, you have wanted to,*
kill me, it would be better. This familiar anger
is enough to leave me barren. I can die in it,
peacefully, and when you lunge, reach to shake
me, I hold you, hold you so tight, hold you
so you can only hold me, and I keep chanting
while we waltz clumsily around the room;
and you, you flame until everything melts to tears,
all this sweaty press of bodies, uncertain muscles,
the sad, sad pain of our bawling, so long
coming, so damned long coming.

RESPITE

All is furtive giggling,
our eyes scanning
the coconut tree-thick shore;
no sign of life.

Lovers now, we embrace
in mid-water, the gentle
ebbing stumbling us;
above the sunlight,

the salt in the air,
a quarrelling shock
of brilliant gulls; our feet
seek firmer footing as we move.

The orgasm comes
like a punch-line,
and our tenderness
is in the daring of it,

the laughter,
the almost drowning
so quickly, so distractingly
delicious.

Away from the long lament –
the tears, the absence of answers,
the realization that distance
and silence, are often the only

healing – my love,

you hold me, fill me
with the peace and constancy
of new homes,

while old homes
seem to crumble about us.
We rest on the beach naked:
sun, flies, sweat, sand, salt

and caresses, giggling.

FOUR

SWITCH

WEATHER

Summer lies — the heat, the flame of its heat,
the streets clotted with shiny-faced black folk
waiting for the bus, waiting in the shade for the bus,
looking bedlamized as any Third World proletariat,
moving slowly with the wisdom of people who understand
the economy of energy preserved. Summer lies
here in South Carolina; it suggests something
tropical — that bland language of a perpetual
season of sameness, no nuance, just flame,
uncompromising flame — but it is a lie.

Seasons change here, and the clouds have nothing
of the swooping hieroglyphs, the twists and flamboyance
of white on startling blue; the air is not
thick with the flirt of food cooking in houses
with wide open windows, wood smoke constant
in the air; and the bodies here slouch along
the roads, spoilt chunkier selves so used
to the caress of manufactured air
and the promise of cooler days.

Further south, the greens are maddening shades,
they drunk you with their language
and the sky's playful tongues dizzy you —
they move quickly, the breezes swirling.

I come home to face that old familiar heat,
my body too long pampered by the debauchery
of a slack regimen. I come to read the signs
in the sky, to pray for healing and truth,
to learn how to decipher the truths of a seasonless

sky — no duplicity here, just the sharp
nakedness of our days, folding one into the other.

Here I must learn, as you have, to count
grace by the hour, by the turn of night into day,
by the quiet repetitions of an island caught
in the muddle of currents, reliable as love.

MIMICS

At dusk here, deep into February, the breeze
canters from the Blue Mountains, licks through
the trees (everything in this city defies
the encroachment of cement) slips softly
through burglar bars and reinforced louvres,
comes cooling on the skin.

In February, the country is counting its dead —
a thousand last season, murdered,
and the simple equation to explain
how cheaply we dispense with life
is cool as these breezes. A man gets drunk
on an island that glows at dusk, fills him
with the nostalgia of an old lover,
the sick taste of her betrayal,
the sweet lingering scent of her embrace.

I arrive in the soft part of the day,
and when you come, having
dallied your way up Old Hope Road
on the eighteen-speed Aunty Flo bequeathed,
I see you balding to a sheen, bearded,
dark and mellow, and I expect you
to be my mirror. Instead you are shorter,
bandy-legged, thinner, more handsome —

this haunting familiarity, as if I know
your body like mine. We embrace.
I linger. Talk is in laughter — it has always been
this way between us. You mimic
old friends, you cast it all in the witticisms

of old Oxford men like our father,
and I know you are shaping a language
for us — our own singular tongue.

I can tell we have mimicked our father, used
his tone, his urbane wit as a buffer
between us — our birthright. Here, together,
it is a trick revealed, another truth
we carry towards each other. So much
has gone before. We remember in code now —
our honed dialect of euphemisms.

Our talk is as gracious as Southern civility,
as cruel as its own rotten past.

You ride into the cool air of February
easy as peas. Tonight the dogs relay.
Every sound has its own discourse.
I will sleep and perhaps dream of you:
man now, grown man, now, riding through
this bloody city, enacting a miracle
in each safe arrival at your destination
on your road-worn bicycle.

SWITCH

I did not come this time to find you. I came
clouded by my own laments. When I was spoken to,
I stayed dumb — my silence, the deep sorrow
of facing my ugliness, the callous abuse
of misplaced affections. Oh the things I have written!
The blue streak of debauchery I have uttered!

I found you so steady in your remission, I was
envious. I grew impatient at your rituals
of self-pity, but you offered them as a gesture
of love, the familiar code of people who
have learned the ritual roles of blame
and guilt. You were half-hearted at it this time.

We have always known that your
suffering and my assurances are requisite
to this love. This time, seeing me
out-depress you, it may have frightened you,
and it certainly stumped you dumb.

It rained in Kingston that night, quick bursts
that left Molynes Road flooded,
the streets glimmering with the large
pools of collected water. Sunday night,
and Half-Way-Tree was jumping with brilliant
light and the rapid sound of DJs.

Something has changed: my tender,
beaten-up body, so guilt-wracked,
is a new continent for our love, a foreign land
whose language we are learning to speak.

LADY BEE

Lady Bee is dead — that disease devoured him.
He lasted almost a year, then he died. Perhaps
the ribbons of tongues burst on his lips, aflame
in the ward. He broke into tongues like that
on the parade ground, his prayers in the midst
of the most ordinary acts. I did not know then
that it was his prayer-language, the tongue
of prophecy, the Holy Ghost in his heart
that took him when he least expected it: Love.

He is dead now, the Captain, the lanky
officer who sprinted brilliantly, but like a girl,
a strong, elemental girl who leaned and wind-
milled his arms on the turns before the eighty
yards home — perhaps negotiating the physics
of the Lord's voice in his head. Captain was
kind, a good guy, but he could not have
heard the Spirit that night when I found you,
and you whispered to me with your eyes —
so full of stones, questions, answers,
dreams, mysteries, shocks — that you could
fly, that you could read my mind, that you
could fly. No tongues hurled forward so I would
know what they had done to you — no Spirit
spoke. Everyone, Captain, too, was dumb.
Captain was Lieutenant then, then he climbed
to Captain, and later Major — I call him *Captain* still,
it suits him, how I trusted him then, captain, my captain.

He kept climbing. The Lord prospered him
in this world of miniature achievement,
while you stayed buck-private. Of course,

you had your triumphs: you flew and sometimes tongues
would flare from you and we all looked around
for someone to translate — though no one did, not then,
not a single soul spoke, not friends,
not the good Captain in his Sam Browns
and burnished boots, with his swanky
salute and clipped eyes-rights.

Today, you carry the news of the captain's passing.
Lady Bee is dead, you say with sadness; you tell me
it is a good thing he was ready — that they say he
spoke in tongues before his eyes rolled back
in reverie. I think of you as a saint, now;
the way you announce his end with love.

AFTER "INHERITANCE"

You wrote "Inheritance" forgetting that a poem
is a prophecy and the first curse will fall on the poet

who speaks it. You wrote as if you did not know
that words have this way of turning on you.

You paint pictures thinking you have mastered
empathy, the capacity to see into what lies

outside of you, when you have merely learned
to read your own story, the tea leaves, the tyrant

that shows its hand in small dollops — little morsels
of terrible pain. Today you've become that drunken

prodigal poet stumbling into his art on the beach,
but you have no beach and your art seems

so insignificant and petty. Instead you have
the dark taste of death on your tongue,

and for once, you understand the love of rum —
or some numbing thing that will make

you fall into a stupor. Your goatish years
are unfruitful acts of idiocy, and love

cracks at home. It is hard to not see
the patterns of a long tragic night,

how at dawn she will discover that something
has died in her. These lessons to a poet

have come too late and now you write with no
epiphany, just the dreary cadence of regret.

FAT MAN

How terrible the confession, *We are all dying*.
The way fat weighs us and the heart swells
from too long labouring to make us breathe, slouch
and snore with guttural dreadfulness (the terror
of it). I do not want to die. So absurd
this admission, this effort to confront
the unpredictable odds of our living. But fat
people die sooner – we know this – and I,
too, too solid with the mess of casualness,
grow fat with age. So hard to come back.
I stare at my stranger self in hotel mirrors.
I am afraid to meet this stomach-glorious
creature, unable these days to find an angle
of satisfying grace. I am now a circle of errors;
the fat has taken over. Perhaps pride in this
plump existentialism will make it well,
but my child seems too, too small,
helplessly small in my clumsy arms.
They, my children, will call me fat,
and I will resent their kindnesses
and compensations for my limp and waddle.
I dream of sweat, the familiar
hint of muscles beneath the inner flesh,
the rib, a reminder of the body
so vulnerable beneath this cloak of flesh.
I dream of breathing easily when I bend
to tie my shoelaces. I dream
of better days when I will leap lightly,
a slender man gambolling in the mirror's face.

ALMA MATER

At the gentrified end of Hope Road before the suburban
foothills, beyond the spear-point, blue-and-white wrought
iron fence, beyond the sentinel ficus berry trees, their massive
spread shadowing the gates, beyond the gray chapel now
stripped bare of its tendrils of ivy, leaving deep grey raw
cement walls pocked with once ornate cubbyholes and webbed
by dry vines – this grey, a hundred years of grey like old skin
uncovered – somewhere on the crescent road, I lost my way,
lost myself, and now I am not sure who I am.

Truths come in well-worn clichés: I am looking for myself.
It is so simple to construct a myth of one's life – these narratives
are tyrants; the parade of characters lock you into a way
of seeing yourself and soon you learn of how lost
you are. I return to the blown-out windows, the crumbling
facades, the peeling walls, the distended edifices of my old
school where I first thought I knew myself. Everything
is ruined here, and I grow sad – nothing is permanent.

On the front wall of the old Physics lab, I find the fading
colours of a mural of footballers I painted twenty-five
years ago. I had forgotten it, but there it stands like a clue
to something. (These days I study old photos of me,
trying to remember what age looks like by staring at youth.)
There it is: crude, uncertain art. This is the last true sign
of neglect: that it is still there, that no one thought
it worth the time to send boys up ladders to repaint it,
cover it, restart with new skin. Were it a gesture
of preservation – something honouring the art – I would
have been flattered, but these walls have not been
painted in thirty years. I grow dizzy from the turning
shadows of the immortelle tree.

I am eleven again, bewildered by the novelty
of a new school, my eyes trying to drink it in,
my body unsure of its meaning, its possibility;
at the cusp of something new, feeling
that familiar fear of myself, making
my first decision there – to change my name, not
Neville any more, not the Anglo name, the protection
of my father's birthright, his Oxbridge imprimatur,
not the name I wore to fend off the vicious jokes
about skinny, big-nosed African boys – not Neville
any more. I declare my new name – that old name
I have turned to all my life: Kwame. I feel its mother-
tongue rolling out of me, that flat Akan weightiness,
and I hear its echo in the voices of children – a small
epiphany, a small narrative, a small myth, a legend.

Now, thirty years later, I am listening
for the reassuring echo of my name
across the bare school-yard. I have come for this,
I think. First there is this deep silence; it stretches
across everything, then settles dumbly on me.

DREAM: BUSHING

Your face, your glowing forehead, the sharp line
of your cheek, your dark nails, the thin vein

that wraps around your arm, the flimsy shirt
that clings to your chest, the tentative giddiness

of your laughter trying to feel me out; the fact
that you want to say *love*, to reach across to me

and embrace, to reach into time to find our history
of affinity during those years when we were, despite

the five years separating us, twins, a pair, roommates.
This moment, like all dreams, turns in me that hunger

to find the calming vacuum where unformed words
can slip out, slowly – the dizzying ooze of language.

It is about love, isn't it? I want to love you
in that most selfish way, so horribly futile

yet so satisfying. These dreams leave me tender,
my skin prickling with the wash of recognition,

and in their wake is the detritus of a tortured land,
an open field of shredded yellow petals and bleeding

grass. I am left bare, vulnerable and shell-shocked.
We should have held each other without letting go.

ON THE BIRTH OF MY SON
For Kekeli

No sharp screams, although after they lifted him,
his brown body covered in the soft film of clay,
he thumped the air and made sounds.
They plucked him out from ribbons of flesh,
the neat line in her skin, with the chord
taut around his neck. And it was only in that
instant of limbs, umbilicus, slick hair
and the glare of the OR's blue light,
the crowd in green uniforms around us,
that I knew that the fluttering in my chest
was not from the trauma, the rush, the sprint
to extract him breathing, alive, it was
the revelation of his penis, the sound
of the word, *son*, its alien sobering, and the rush
of every image, every fear, every silence,
every tension, every broken meaning.

MY LITTLE BROTHER
For Lisa

Perhaps this is the way of siblings, the younger
locked in that infant self – the ideal place

of memory. Your manhood, so startling to me,
is an ordinary fact but I slip sometimes and call you

my little brother. Thirty-odd years and I carry
this language of protection. I speak to you

as if you have not left that teenager's giddy
place of wonder and hope; looking ahead

for time to make of you a future. Time obliged,
but who can blame us for not getting the joke.

You fight back. There is a child you have
seeded who looks up at her father – tall,

grand, ancient as her fledgling memory allows;
and sometimes I see you chasing

that girl who sprints away in a swirl of her golden
frock, her laughter a trail of bright petals,

as she leaps over the hills of St. Ann; the sea
at her back, and you giddy, keeping pace behind.

.

FIVE

MISTAKE

MISTAKEN

A man mistook me for you.
He wrote a letter; asked if I was the one
that went berserk at a camp in the hills.

In his remembering, the boy
standing in the mud despite the sudden
glare of an after-rain sky, watching

the other boys, near men, play-acting warriors,
eyes hot with the conviction of such
rituals – screaming their commands,

you defiant, unwilling to play along.
He wrote to me twenty years later as if
he was still the eleven year old who never

learned if the silent creature, laugh-less
and dull-eyed who stumbled from the cage
they kept him in for a night and a day,

was fine, was okay – he wrote as if
he could never shake the clatter
of it all; the sound of a teenager,

his voice just breaking, howling through
the night; the frogs bleating, the wind
crying, the older boys joking, and everyone

forgetting how easily boys become
killers, how easily blood makes men
of us. He said he was glad to see

I was doing so well – such success.
My survival – *your* survival – was his healing.
So when I wrote to say that I was not

who he thought I was; when I said
your mind had unhinged that night,
that your life had stopped for seven years,

that everything stopped growing; when I wanted
him to know of my guilt for not seeing
that someone did this to you; that *they* did this

to you; that it was not weed, not the trauma
of a last child, not envy, not some
diabolic demon, but the brute cruelty

of boys coaxed by pathetic men, so impotent
that they sought to relive their failed
lives in the company of boys;

when I told him all this, he never
wrote back, not once, not again.

ACKNOWLEDGEMENTS

Several of these poems first appeared, often in different guises, in *New and Selected Poems* (Peepal Tree Press, 2003).

Thanks to the Dawes family for giving me permission to be a poet, the freedom and the space to be so. Special thanks to Cave Canem for being a welcoming home for many of these poems. Thanks to Charlene Spearen and Ellen Arl for their eyes and their constant encouragement. Thanks to the USC Department of English for making the space for me to continue to pursue this craft.

'Legend' was selected as one of the best poems of the year and published in *The Forward Book of Poetry 2007*.

PRAISE FOR *IMPOSSIBLE FLYING*

Kwame Dawes is one of the most important writers of his generation who has built a mighty and lasting body of work. *Impossible Flying* is surely his finest book of poetry thus far. These poems are both distilled and richly colored. They synthesize rage, grief, pragmatism, and beauty into a love axis so deeply felt and powerfully expressed it startles.

– Elizabeth Alexander
Yale University

In *Impossible Flying*, Kwame Dawes brings Auden's dictum to mind: 'We must love one another or die.' Dawes confronts death, madness, grief and loss with the power of compassion, a fierce determination to honor his family and his beloved Jamaica. The poet's language is vivid and visceral; his courage and honesty blaze a path in poem after poem. This is the music of survival and transcendence. Indeed, the poetry of Kwame Dawes makes the impossible possible.

– Martín Espada

Majestic is the word that comes to mind reading the finely wrought poems of Kwame Dawes' *Impossible Flying*. Indeed, a sublime talent is needed to fashion poems of such capacious grace and energy. They are simultaneously intimate and political, intellectual and blood-filled, elegiac and enraptured: human in the most epic sense. No other poet of Dawes' generation is writing poems this relevant, this revelatory.

– Terrance Hayes

Impossible Flying is Kwame Dawes's most intimate collection to date. The poems are a conversation with his familial past, present and the impending future – of good and sad memories, of births, deaths, and illnesses, of loneliness and intimacies. But above all, it is poetry about relationships of all kinds – not just between family members, but variant selves, identities, and masks. The evocative birth of his son emerges beautifully as a "brown body covered in the soft film of clay", couched ambitions "whispered about being superheroes and flying" flutter in a Hounslow basement, and reflections on "the way fat weighs us and heart swells" are just few examples of Dawes's phrase-making that is always honest, sharp, and deeply resonant.

Impossible Flying flies through territories most poets are not willing to visit – it makes what might be impossible for many, possible for some. Ultimately, the strength of this book lies not only in its exactitude of language and tonality, but also in the way vulnerability is presented in an unapologetic, convincing, and moving manner. The over-coolness of contemporary English poetry can learn a lot from Dawes's lyrical bass-tuned pitch, sermonic narrative style, and intelligent range.

– Sudeep Sen, author of *Postmarked India: New & Selected Poems* (HarperCollins)

EXTRACTS FROM REVIEWS OF EARLIER COLLECTIONS

Progeny of Air
ISBN: 9780948833687 £7.99

The book extends across a wide range of experiences, its first section focusing on incidents from childhood and adolescence. Many of these poems convey the painful cruelty of children, the pecking order of threat and coercion, terrible rites of passage. The playwright's skills of strong characterization are evident in the 'Hall of Fame', a series of vignettes of various characters, pupils and masters. The teachers are portrayed as figures of power and influence, but Dawes is aware of their off-duty lives too, striving to paint the whole picture. These portraits are invigorating and compassionate, suggesting that these men had futures as well as pasts, just like the boys on the threshold of adulthood. This is only one example of the way Dawes often offers a very different perspective on quite ordinary things, implying that time is more than simply a chronological device, and that culture and society is more than the hierarchy imposed upon 'the disorder of our terrible existence'. ... Dawes revels in the 'freedom to write the hidden'

He takes many admirable risks, borrowing narrative techniques from the story-telling tradition and rhythms from reggae. His vocabulary is a curious mixture of formal precise or prosaic words together with street slang and surprising compounds, all informed by a love of traditional 'English' poetry instilled at school in Jamaica - 'the jazz of words against words / making beauty in rhythm, sound, in twisted / clash of constructs we did not really grasp // but felt...'

I am grateful to Kwame Dawes for writing this book and bringing some heat to a grey and chilly autumn; grateful also to the Forward panel of judges for awarding it their First Collection Prize and so bringing it to the attention of a wider audience. Peepal Tree are bringing out two further books. I look forward to seeing what else this man can do.

Linda France *Poetry Review*

Prophets

ISBN: 9780948833854 £8.99

Dawes fuses charisma and comment, imagination and documentary, invoking elements from the genre of popular culture, sub-culture, Jamaican ethos and song, effectively and lyrically. The aspects of lyricism and song are crucial to the carriage of the book's narrative. Song works in multiple ways – as praise, as penance, as pursuant of peace, as provider of pleasure. Song is also rhythm, and rhythm is reggae – indigenous, pure, full of bass resonance - which quietly provides not only a chorus leit-motif but also the syllabic markers that anchor the overall scale and story. Clarice and Thalbot who play the role of the protagonists of this arching operatic tale are dextrously cast.

Kwame Dawes' may elicit comparisons with 'novels-in-verse' or 'poems-as-narrative novel', especially with works such as Vikram Seth's *The Golden Gate*, Derek Walcott's *Omeros*, Craig Raine's *History: The Home Movie*, or even King James' version of The Bible. If comparisons have to be made, they ought to be done setting one thing absolutely clear, that here is one writer who writes out of his own tissue, with intelligence, originality, and passion, employing his very own idiom. If there are influences, then the most likely tints of the spectrum would include Walcott, Bob Marley, Christianity, colonialism, but all of these obliquely and indirectly. *Prophets* is a major book, a feast of spontaneity set in a serious framework. It is a narrative poem of sheer power, contemporaneity, and hope; one that is full of beauty, sadness, wisdom, and true humanism.

Sudeep Sen

Requiem

ISBN: 9781900715072

Kwame Dawes' *Requiem* and *Jacko Jacobus* reveal a fresh talent, ready to take his place as one of the finest poets who has emerged during the 1990's. Like his two great compatriots, Derek Walcott and Kamau Brathwaite who, undoubtedly, represent the best tradition of Caribbean poetry, Dawes is similarly committed to capturing the essence of the Caribbean islands in expressions of compelling lyricism.

In *Requiem*, a work whose inspiration is derived from the illustrations of American artist, Tom Feeling's award-winning work, The Middle Passage: White Ships/Black Cargo, Dawes relies on the lyric form of the elegy to recreate the pain of suffering of slavery, and the possibility of redemption.

Indeed, in 'Requiem', the title poem, a lament for the many casualties of transatlantic slavery on the one hand and a celebration of hope on the other, the poet-persona reveals that he hears 'a blue note/ of lament, sweet requiem/for the countless dead,/ skanking feet among shell,/coral, rainbow adze,/webbed feet, making as if/to lift, soar, fly into new days'. In 'Vultures', the poet finds an apt metaphor for the beneficiaries - in the purely commercial sense - of the inhuman crime of slavery: 'These vultures speckle a blue sky/and learn the trade routes/ to the castles by the sea…' The gloom conveyed to the reader by the threnodic import of Dawes' imagery is remarkably tempered by a sense of hope, life, of survival, freedom: 'We sing laments so old, so true/then straighten our backs again.'

The technical accomplishment of Kwame Dawes' poetry is indicative of his ability to maintain a cool air while employing the genre of the lyric to explore his themes, and to cultivate an economy of expression while striving to maintain high quality in deployment of imagery.

Idowu Omoyele

Jacko Jacobus
ISBN: 9781900715065

The Caribbean is finding a big new voice of alarm in Kwame Dawes. *Jacko Jacobus* is a long rollickingly control biographical-political-erotical epic — a novel in two-line verse-form almost — but always a poem — inspire by that most socially intriguing of Old Testament Bible 'prophets', the story of Jacob & Esau
Already I hear this on radio, on CD, see it in flim & video
Where nex to, Jacko

Kamau Brathwaite

Shook Foil
ISBN: 9781900715140

Few poets capture the mood of a generation. In *Shook Foil*, Kwame Dawes, 'drawing on inspiration as diverse as Derek Walcott, T. S. Eliot and Lorna Goodison,' attempts to define reggae and the major personality behind the success of the music, Bob Marley... who taught my generation how to be Jamaican and Pan-African (as if the two terms were mutually exclusive), how to honor ourselves and others, and finally how to love.

Throughout the collection, Dawes captures the many dimensions of reggae from the psalmic to the prophetic that are yet to be explored by other writers and musicians. Reggae remains unparalleled in its ability to absorb other influences and remain true to itself and to capture beauty, pain, and pleasure in a one-drop riddim. Its syncopation suggests a break, a gap – somewhere to fall with the faith that you will be caught – and this is what gives reggae its redemptive value. To really enjoy the music, you must believe. The same could be said of *Shook Foil*

Geoffrey Philp *The Caribbean Writer*

New and Selected Poems
ISBN: 9781900715706 £9.99

In what seems a very short time, Kwame Dawes has established a reputation as a poet and critic of an unusually wide-ranging and sympathetic intelligence... One has a sense, reading over Dawes's work, that his is an active intelligence in the best tradition of the practitioner-critic, the different facets of his work – poetry, drama, public reading, reviewing, interviews with other Caribbean writers and academic criticism – each serving to inform his overall artistic project.

This is poetry dancing to a different drummer: the range of reference, the cultural assumptions bound into the poems, the cast and turn of the language, the lyrical drive... all of these announce another way of thinking about 'poetry in English', where both 'poetry' and 'English' are problematic terms to be challenged and redefined.

Stewart Brown *Poetry Review*

ALSO BY KWAME DAWES

A Far Cry from Plymouth Rock: A Personal Narrative
ISBN 9781845230258 £12.99

After ten years of living and working in South Carolina, of trying to manage a writing career that spans the USA, the UK and Jamaica, but of hanging onto a Ghanaian passport despite its manifold inconveniences at airport immigration desks, the question of where was home had become for Kwame Dawes ever more insistent. There is a part of him that embraces the New World condition of being Kamau Brathwaite's 'poor, harbourless spade', but America has entered his psyche; he writes poems filled with the landscapes and racial histories of South Carolina, and yet the thought of becoming an American citizen is almost too uncomfortable to contemplate.

In this deeply personal narrative, Dawes explores the experiences that bring him to this state of indecision. At its heart lies his relationship with his father, Marxist, Caribbean nationalist, writer, a relationship Dawes has explored in manifold forms in his fiction and poetry, and which in this book he approaches directly for the first time. In the process, he writes with great thoughtfulness about place (Ghana, Jamaica, Canada, the UK and South Carolina), about race, nation, religion, childhood, family and parenthood, sex and death.

As a writer, and as a husband, father, teacher, churchgoer and community activist, and one sees that for Dawes the page and the world, cannot be divided. If, in the end, there is a conclusion, it is about embracing the abrasions and joys of difference. In a world where the pressures to homogenise are so great, one realises just how important it is that there are writers like Kwame Dawes around.

All Peepal Tree titles are available from our website: www.peepaltreepress.com; email orders@peepaltreepress.com Or you can contact us at Peepal Tree Press, 17 Kings Avenue, Leeds LS6 1QS, UK (Tel +44 113 245 1703)